Nicolas Vadot

THE GEORGE W BUSH YEARS

"I'm the master of low expectations."
—George W Bush, aboard Air Force One, June 4, 2003

Before becoming president, **George Walker Bush** hadn't done a lot of travelling. Once elected—with fewer votes than his opponent—he mistook Slovakia for Slovenia, thought the inhabitants of Greece were called *Greekians* and didn't know the name of Pakistan's Prime Minister. And to him *Bin Laden* was probably an East German car brand. Nevertheless, as months went by, he made a lot of progress in geopolitics, realising for instance that the Afghan mountains were packed with people like him, therefore he wasn't the only religious fundamentalist on Earth. Of course, after eight years in power, he still has trouble distinguishing a Shiite from a Sunni, a Kurd or even a European. However, what he does now know is that on the other side of the Atlantic Ocean, on the right-hand side of Britain, lies an *Old Continent*, full of pacifist beatniks who speak several languages and who have all abolished the death penalty. In other words: true savages. He can still hardly tell the difference between a nice little morning breeze and a devastating hurricane and doesn't know what a weapon of mass destruction *really* looks like, but he's eager to fill the gaps in his general knowledge during his third term.

What?? He can't run for a third term?? What a pity...

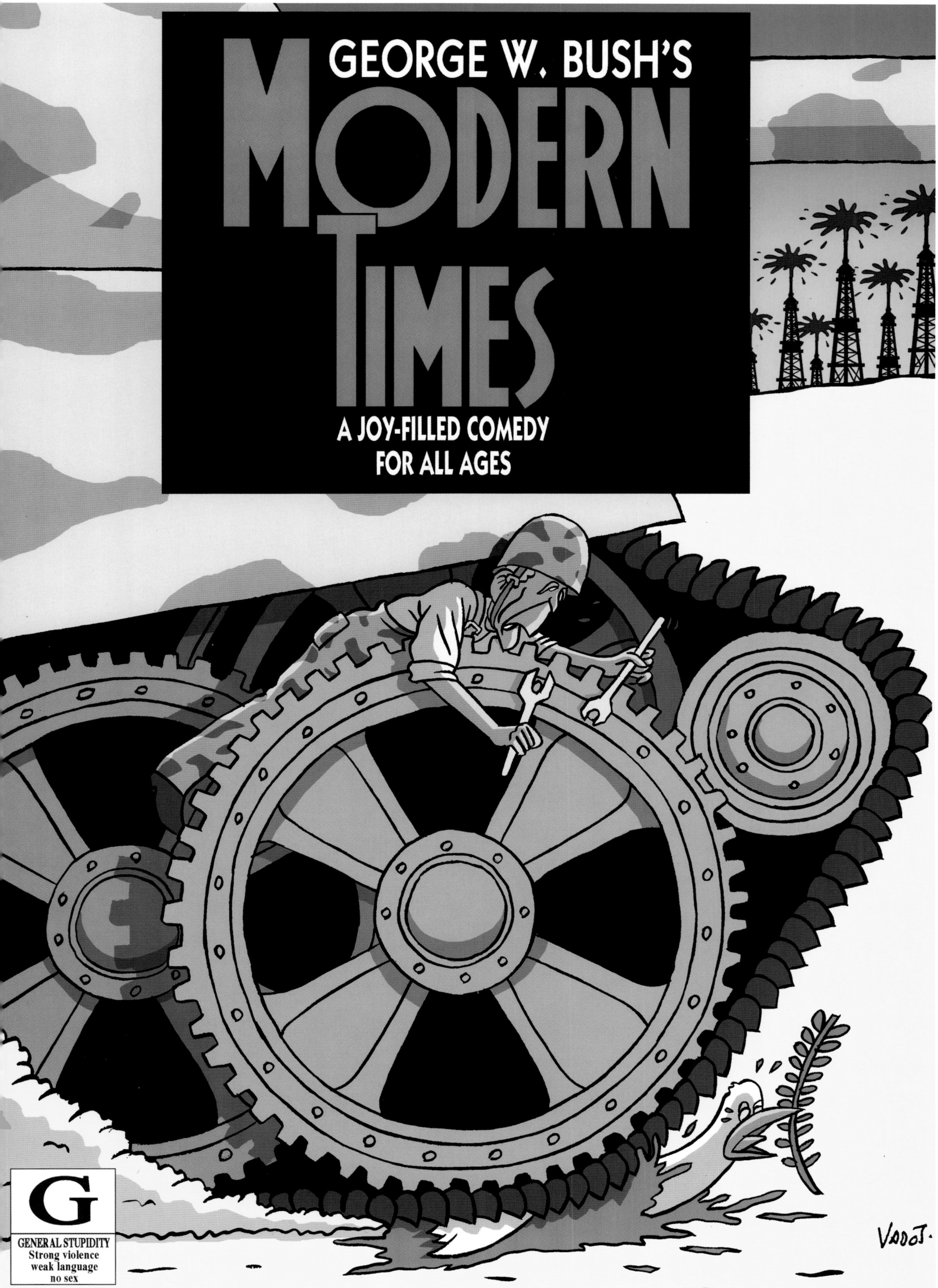
GEORGE W. BUSH'S
MODERN TIMES
A JOY-FILLED COMEDY
FOR ALL AGES
G
GENERAL STUPIDITY
Strong violence
weak language
no sex
VADOT.

Once upon a time in the Far West...

Recount
General confusion during the 2000 American presidential election. Despite having won more votes at the national level and being initially declared the winner, the Democrat candidate Al Gore is finally beaten by George W. Bush. The last state to call is Florida—run by Bush's brother Jeb—where vote-counting machines have proven unreliable, a manual recount is necessary. Bush's presidency starts under serious suspicion.

September 11

Al-Qaeda terrorists hijack four civil airplanes and crash two of them into the World Trade Center in New York City, a third into the Pentagon in Washington. The fourth one—probably en route either to the White House or the Capitol—crashes in Virginia. The September 11 attacks claimed over 3000 lives.

Mixing with the wrong guys
Cold War avatar and Saudi billionaire Osama Bin Laden was used by the
CIA to fight against the Soviet occupation of Afghanistan in the 80's.

BIN LADEN THE TERRORIST IS SUSPECTED OF HAVING TAKEN ADVANTAGE OF FOREIGN TAX HAVENS!

What?! Bin Laden is a terrorist?

What?! There are foreign tax havens?

AL-QAEDA

AL-QAEDA

Tax havens
General questioning about financial networks of terrorist groups such as al-Qaeda.

WORLD ECONOMIC PROSPECTS

Collateral damage
The September 11 attacks could deepen American and worldwide economic recession.

1998   1999   2000   2001

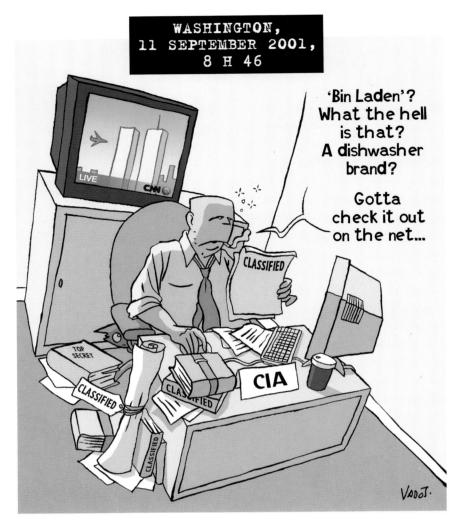

WASHINGTON, 11 SEPTEMBER 2001, 8 H 46

'Bin Laden'? What the hell is that? A dishwasher brand?

Gotta check it out on the net...

CIA
The secret service stands accused of not having foreseen al-Qaeda's emergence and also of not having infiltrated Osama Bin Laden's network in order to thwart the September 11 attacks.

Bin Laden
The al-Qaeda mastermind is hiding in Afghanistan and cannot be found.

We've lost track of Bin Laden: he's **disguised** himself as a woman!

Diplomacy
Europe and UN forces are kept out of
American retaliation plans for Afghanistan.

Great Britain
Despite Europe's reluctance, Prime Minister Tony Blair decides to engage his country alongside the United States in its 'War on Terror', unilaterally declared by George W. Bush.

Afghanistan
Counting on internal destabilisation of the Taliban regime, the United States and their allies support the Afghan Northern Alliance whose leader, Commander Massud, was assassinated on September 9, 2001 by terrorists who passed themselves off as western journalists.

'Operation Enduring Freedom'
Afghanistan: after the bombings, humanitarian aid.

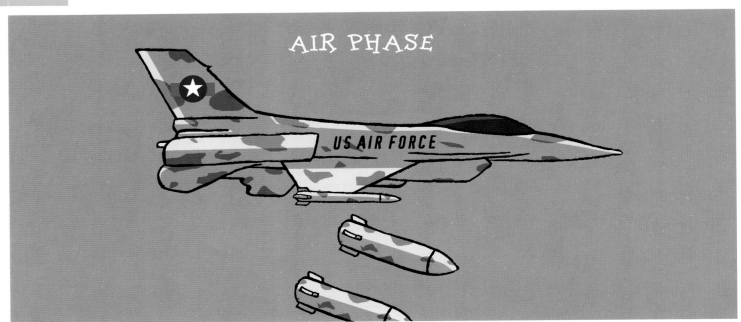

AIR PHASE

LAND PHASE

UNDERGROUND PHASE

Arms
The war in Afghanistan as well as general geopolitical instability threatens the world economies—except expenditure on weapons.

Free trade
World Trade Organisation summit takes place in the Qatari city of Doha, where anti-globalisation protesters gathering from all over the world demonstrate, while the fear of new terrorist attacks is still very high.

2001

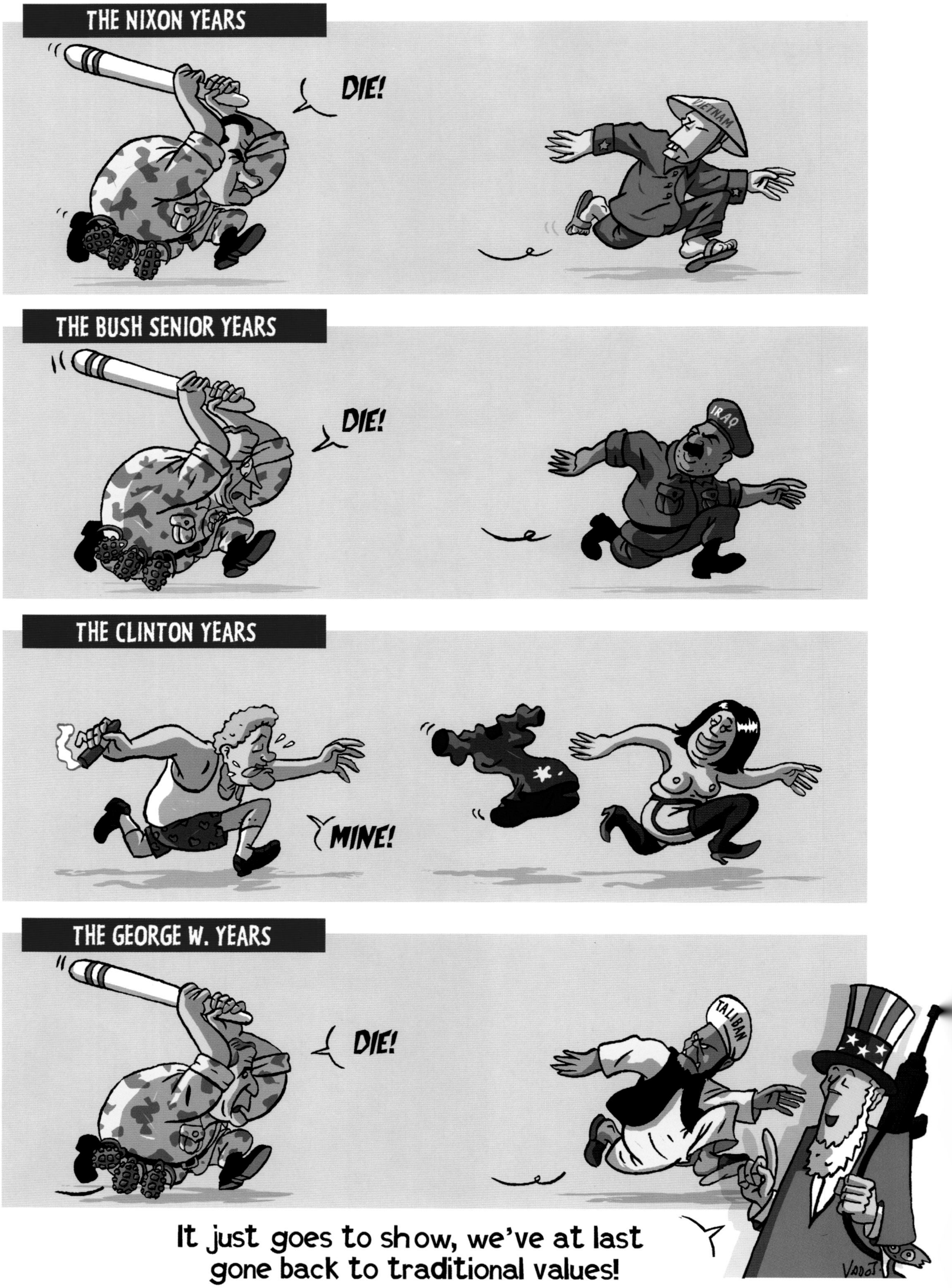

THE NIXON YEARS
DIE!
VIETNAM
THE BUSH SENIOR YEARS
DIE!
IRAQ
THE CLINTON YEARS
MINE!
THE GEORGE W. YEARS
DIE!
TALIBAN
It just goes to show, we've at last gone back to traditional values!

Capitulation
Four months after the September 11 attacks, the Taliban regime is removed from power in Afghanistan, toppled by the Northern Alliance.

And what if, finally, the world was just a village?

You're such a visionary, Mister President!

Chain reaction

Six months after the September 11 attacks, the Bush administration seems to understand at last that the success of its 'War on Terror' is conditional upon a peace solution in the Middle East.

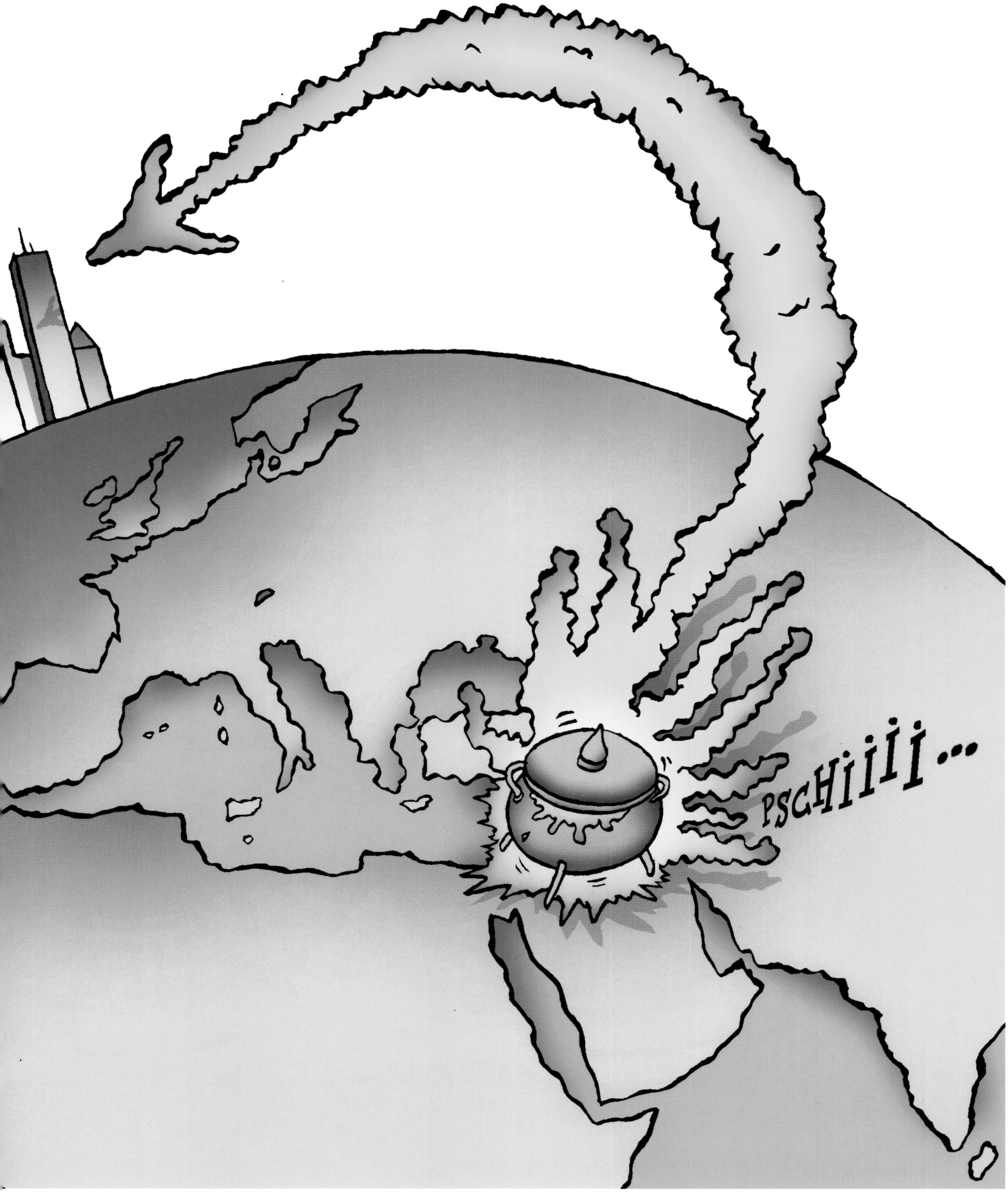
PSCHIIII...

The 'Axis of Evil'
President George W. Bush continues his 'War on Terror', naming Iraq, Iran and North Korea as the three countries representing the Axis of Evil.

Afghanistan
President Ahmed Karzai's Vice-President is assassinated, killed by ethnic infighting.

Daniel Pearl
The *Wall Street Journal* correspondent captured in Pakistan by fundamentalists is found beheaded.

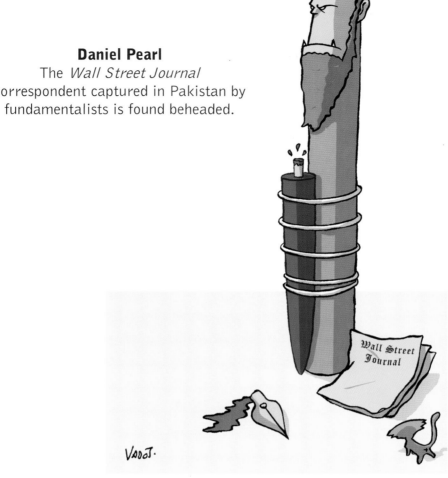

Unilateralism

George W. Bush has great difficulties in convincing his allies to attack Iraq. During the first Gulf War in 1991, his father was able to count on the support of a large international coalition to dislodge Saddam Hussein's troops from invaded Kuwait.

Saddam Hussein

The Iraqi president stands up to the international community and chases out UN's arms inspectors, who were investigating Iraq's military capabilities.

Terrorism

The tracking of al-Qaeda leaders starts paying off: Ramzi Bin al Shibh, one of the 9/11 principal coordinators, is arrested in Pakistan in August 2002. But still no trace of Osama Bin Laden.

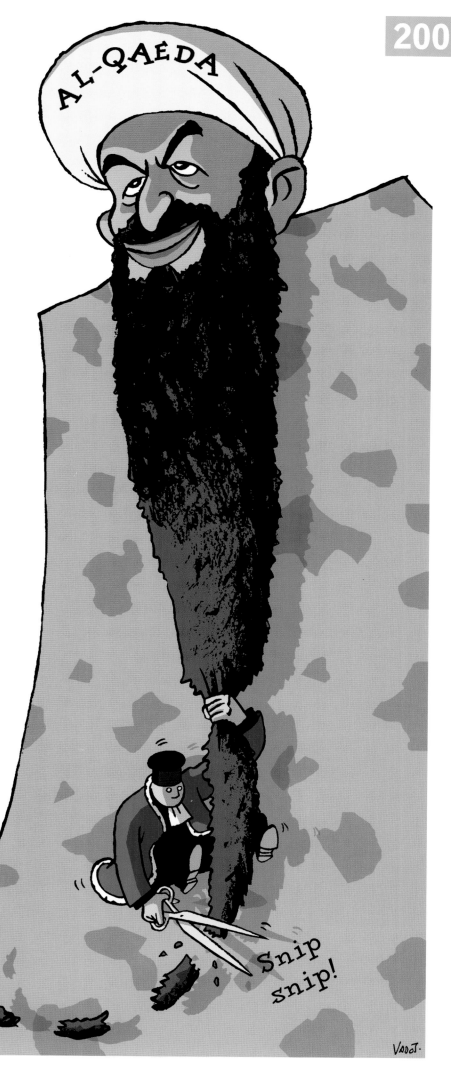

Iraq
George W. Bush wants to get rid of Saddam Hussein, with or without UN approval, even though the Iraqi dictator accepts the return of arms inspectors to his country.

CAMOUFLAGE ART

FRAME 1:
IRAQI
FEEDING
BOTTLES
FACTORY

FRAME 2:
AMERICA
PROTECTING
THE FREE
WORLD

Liars and camouflage
Americans suspect a so-called Iraqi feeding bottles factory to be in fact a manufacturer
of weapons of mass destruction. At the same time, Bush has trouble convincing people
about the real motives that would justify a war against Saddam Hussein's regime.

Nobel Prize

Former American President Jimmy Carter—opposed to a new war in Iraq—receives the Nobel Peace Prize.

The Washington sniper

A mad gunman spreads terror in Washington, hidden in a van, shooting people aimlessly, killing ten. A few weeks later, George W. Bush tries to convince the UN Security Council to adopt a new resolution against Iraq. He's only supported by Great Britain.

Weapons of mass destruction

The 12,000-page report on Iraqi weapons provided by Baghdad to UN arms inspectors is turned down by the Bush administration, which dismisses it as a 'phone book' before even reading it. Troop deployment continues in the Gulf, as if the war were inexorable. Nevertheless, the International Atomic Energy Agency (IAEA) is categorical: Iraq does *not* possess weapons of mass destruction.

Oil slick
The oil tanker *Prestige* sinks off Galicia in Spain.

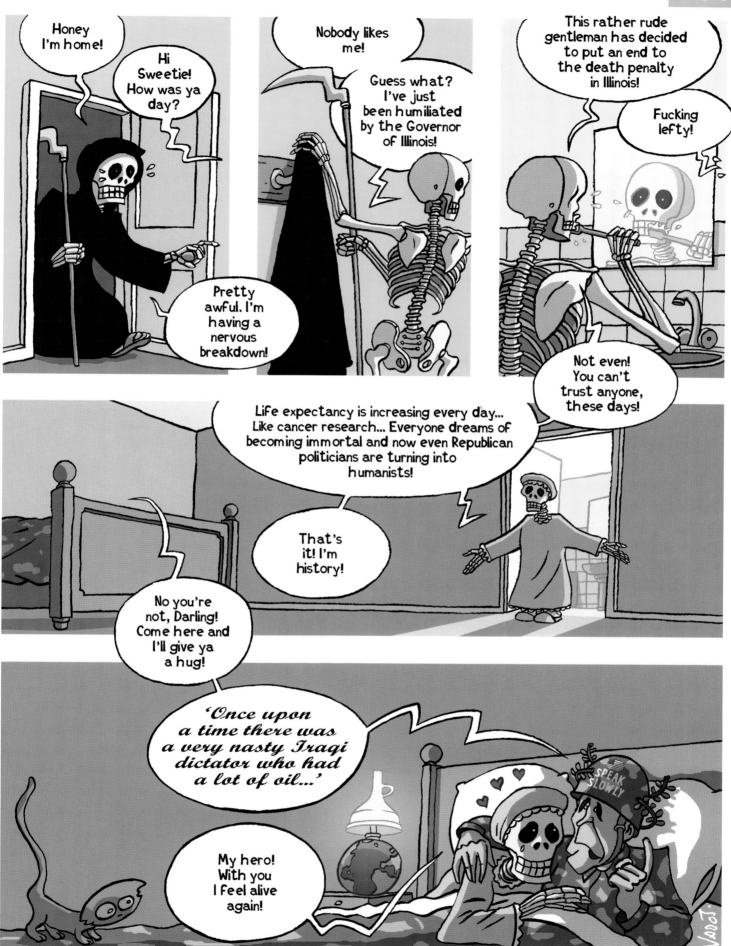

Capital punishment
The Governor of Illinois abolishes the death penalty. Meanwhile, the second Gulf War is imminent.

'Old Europe'
George W. Bush's entourage, especially Defence
Secretary Donald Rumsfeld, denounces the Old
Continent and its wish to avoid a war with Iraq.

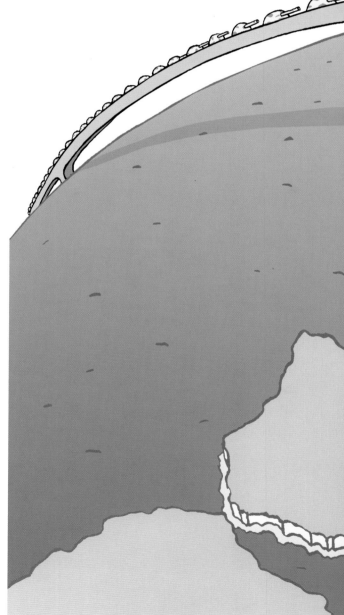

Propaganda
The Bush administration is determined to use the American media as a propaganda weapon to promote its war in Iraq.

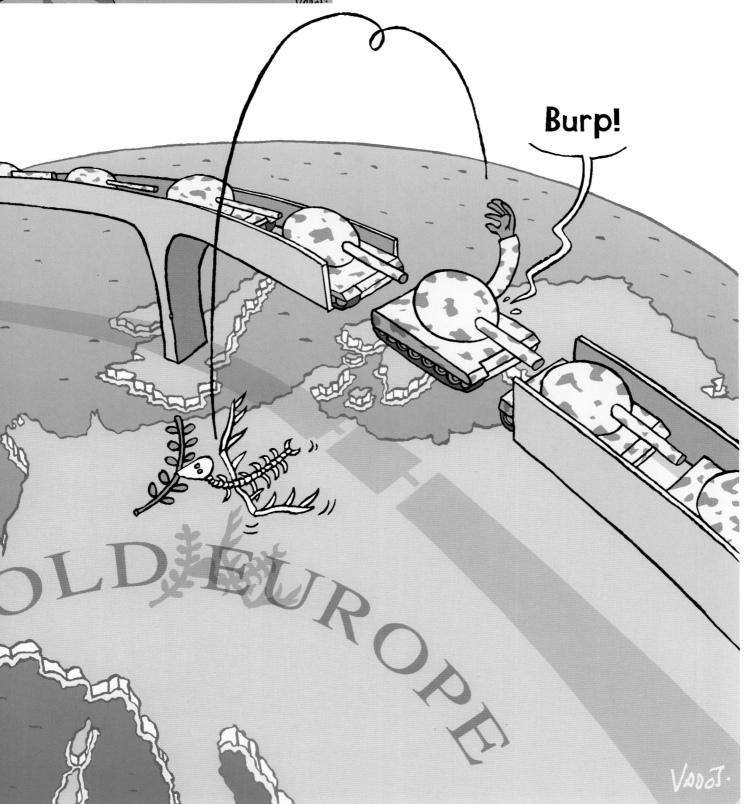

Reconciliation

After fierce debate about the Iraq situation, members of the European Union reach a compromise in order to preserve an appearance of unity, giving more time to UN arms inspectors, without closing the door to the military option as a last resort.

Valentine's Day 2003...

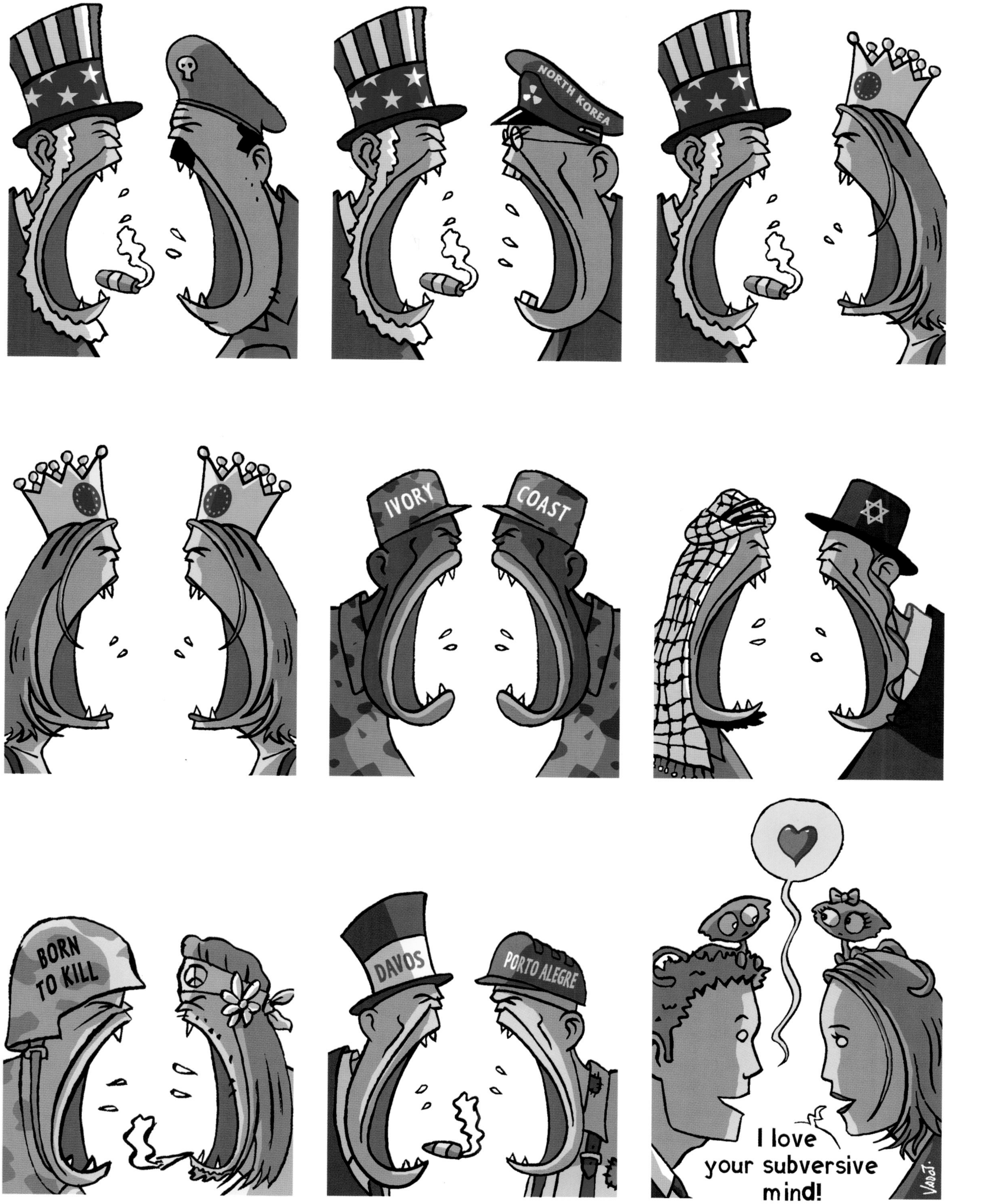
NORTH KOREA
IVORY
COAST
BORN TO KILL
DAVOS
PORTO ALEGRE
I love your subversive mind!

Turk
Ankara opposes the deployment of Americans on its soil. US milit
forces were intending to open a northern front in Ir

8 Marc
International Women's Da

Be afraid...
The American population fears new attacks on its soil as a
result of Islamic retaliation if the United States invades Iraq.

Invasion
17 March 2003: the US-led coalition invades Iraq.

LOOK-ALIKES: BUSH TOO

Double standards

George W. Bush says he wants to push the peace process forward in the Middle East.

Look-alikes

Saddam Hussein seems to be still alive after the American bombings and is seen, radiant, standing in front of supporters. But this could be one of the numerous look-alikes the Iraqi dictator often used in the past.

Guerrilla warfare
Coalition troops are facing first acts of guerrilla warfare from the Iraqi population.

Go it alone
George W. Bush has decided to invade Iraq, without UN approval.

Northern Ireland
Meeting in Belfast between Tony Blair and George W. Bush, who is there to support the peace process between Catholics and Protestants.

Bitter victory
After three weeks of intense and bloody bombing of the civilian population, British and American troops enter Baghdad.

EVERYDAY LIFE IN SOUTH EAST ASIA

SARS

The Severe Acute Respiratory Syndrome (SARS) hits South East Asia, forcing people to wear protection masks in order to avoid infection by the virus. In other news, Saddam Hussein is still at large in Iraq, as well as Osama Bin Laden and Taliban leader Mollah Omar, who escaped on a motorcycle during the American invasion in Afghanistan.

Diplomacy
President Bush rediscovers the UN, asking them to play a major role in Iraq's reconstruction.

Spiral of violence
Deadly attack on UN headquarters in Baghdad. The US and British-led coalition is still faced with a multifaceted Iraqi opposition that is getting more powerful day-by-day.

Suicide
Alastair Campbell, Tony Blair's very influential communications advisor, resigns after the David Kelly scandal. Kelly, a British scientist put under intense pressure for having challenged the British government's allegations regarding the so-called danger of Iraqi weapons, committed suicide a few weeks before.

Mollahs
After Afghanistan and Iraq, it is now the turn of Iran to incur the wrath of Washington because of its nuclear programme.

Middle East
Three years after the start of the Second Intifada in Palestine,
the conflict has already claimed more than 3000 lives.

Reversal

One year prior to the next Presidential election, American public opinion is starting to express doubts about the Bush administration's policy in Iraq.

Carnage

A missile launched by the Iraqi militia hits a US Air Force helicopter in Fallujah, killing 16 soldiers.

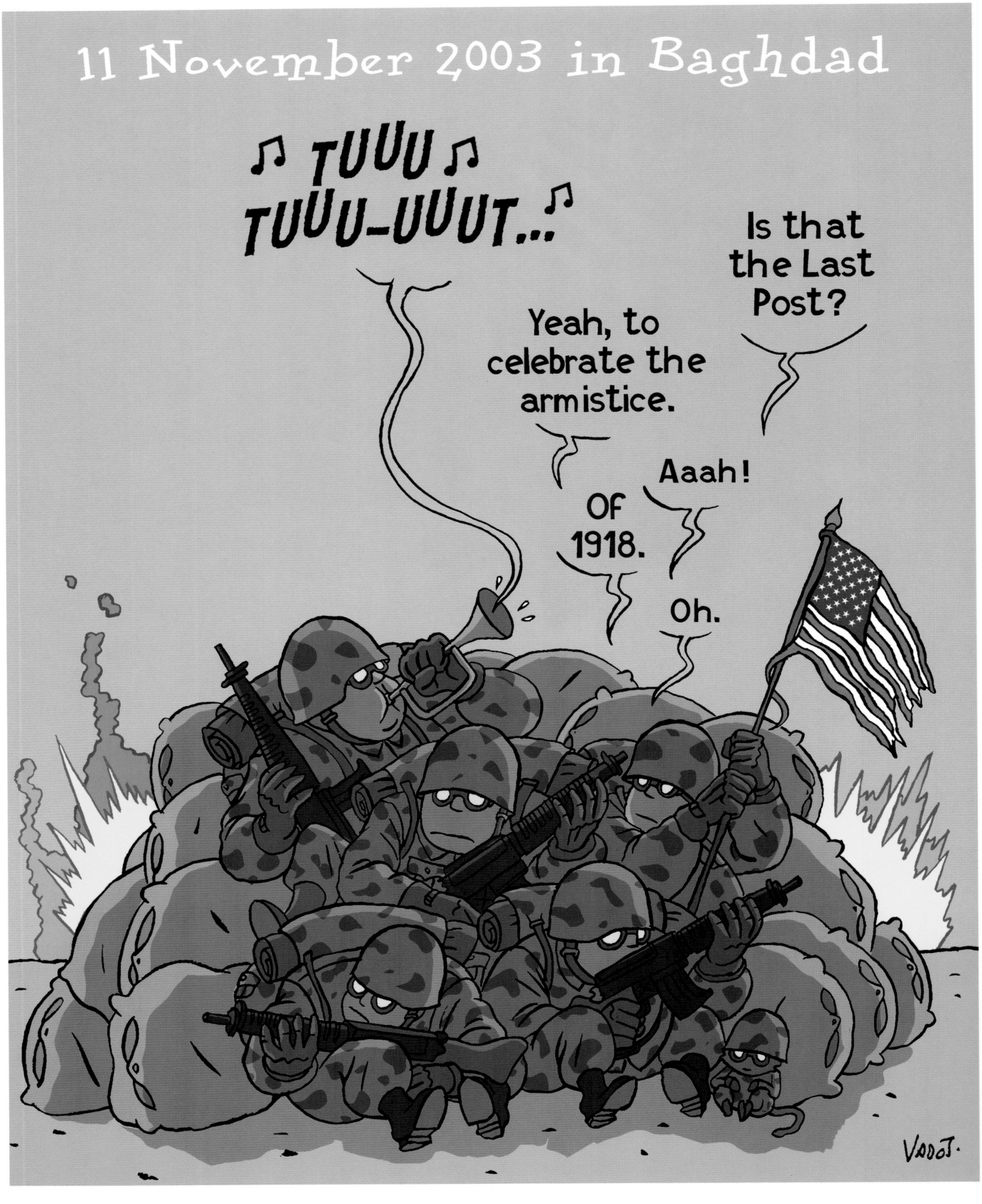
11 November 2003 in Baghdad
♫ TUUU ♫ TUUU-UUUT..♫
Is that the Last Post?
Yeah, to celebrate the armistice.
Aaah!
Of 1918.
Oh.
VADOT.

Nihilism
An al-Qaeda-led terrorist attack claims the lives of 17
people in Riyadh, Saudi Arabia. All victims are Muslims.

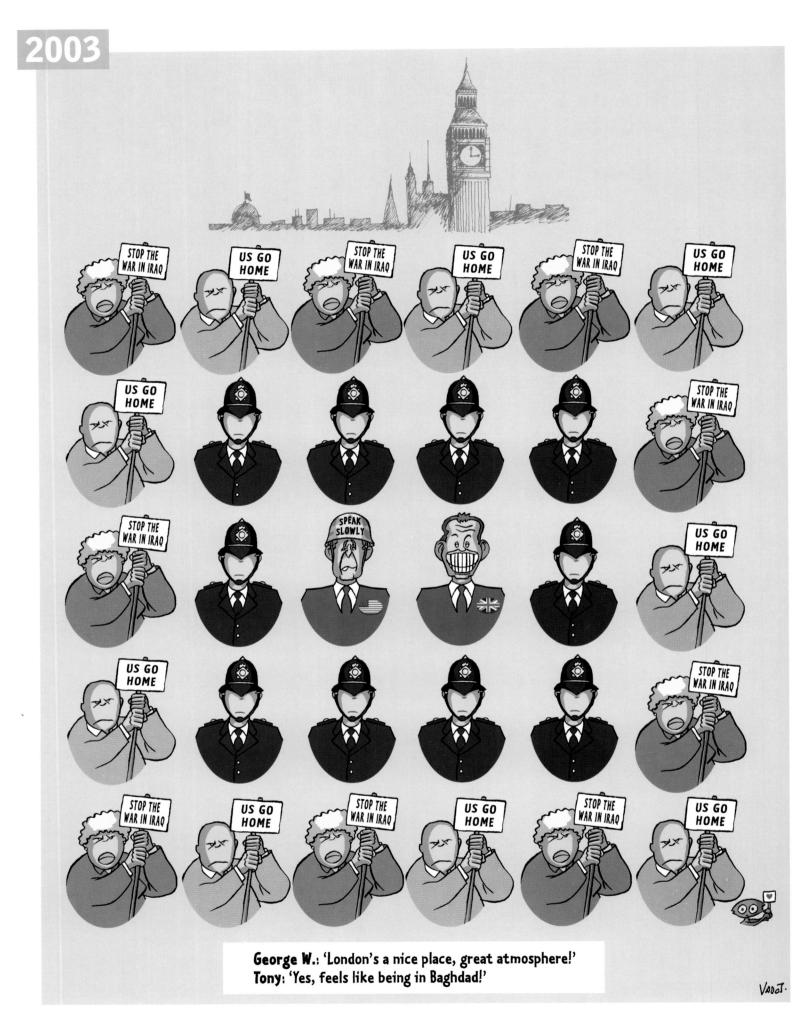

George W.: 'London's a nice place, great atmosphere!'
Tony: 'Yes, feels like being in Baghdad!'

Tea for two
High security trip to London for George W. Bush,
discussing an exit plan from Iraq with his ally Tony Blair.

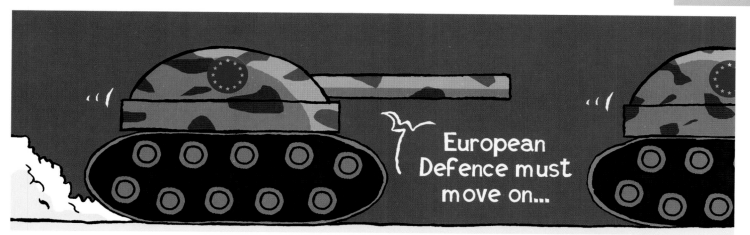

Europe
France, Germany and Great Britain outline a European defence project, without much room for manoeuvre. The Americans don't want the Old Continent's initiative to overshadow NATO.

'We got him!'
Despite having found no weapons of mass destruction in
Iraq, Americans manage to capture Saddam Hussein,
showing footage of the deposed dictator, unshaven and
haggard, being examined by a coalition doctor.

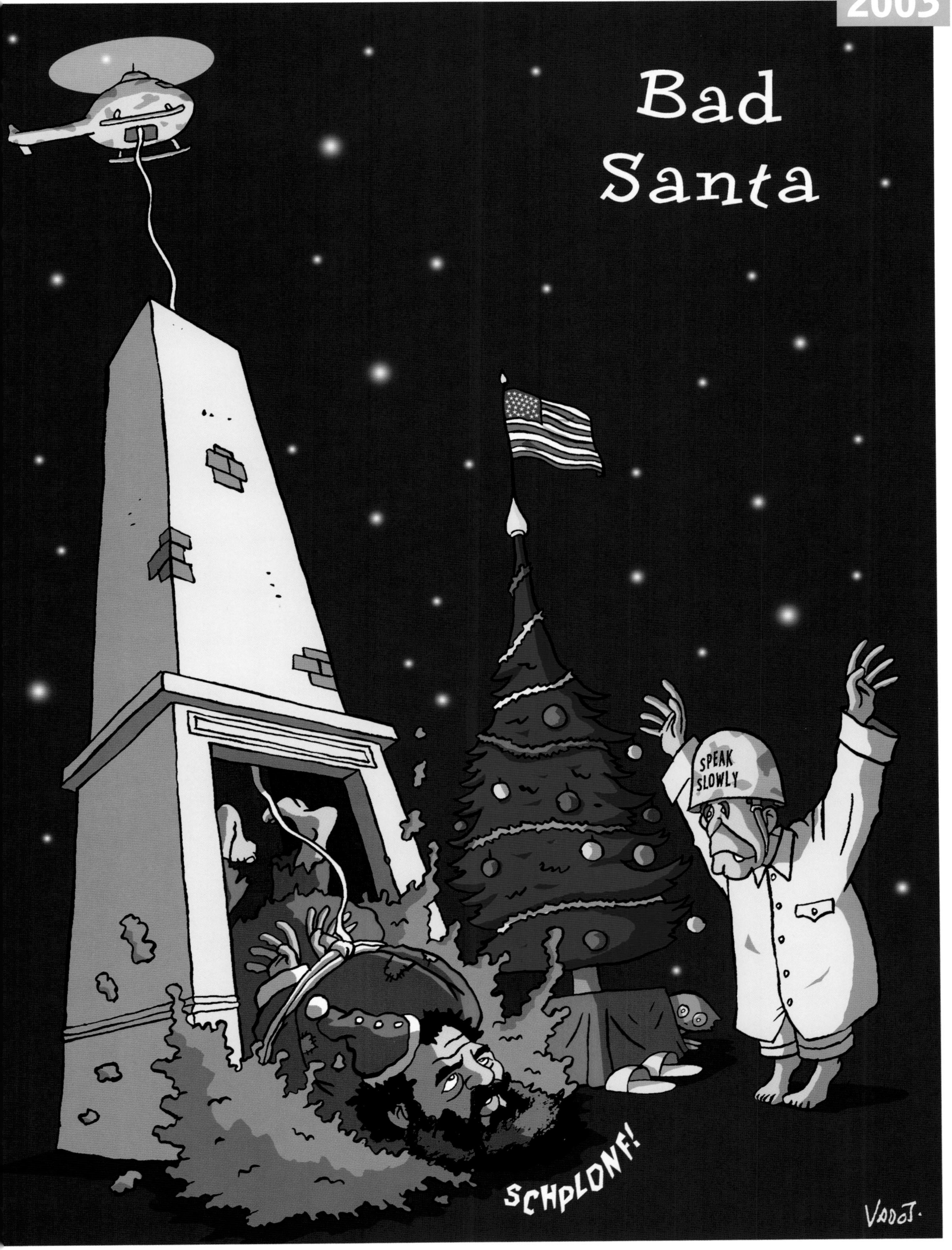
Bad Santa
SPEAK SLOWLY
SCHPLONF!
VADOT.

Man on the Moon
Bush says he wants his country to put Americans on the Moon again shortly. Meanwhile, American headquarters in Baghdad is targeted by a suicide attack with 24 dead, mostly Iraqis.

John Kerry
The senator from Massachusetts will be the Democrat candidate for the forthcoming Presidential election against George W. Bush, who calls an election earlier than expected, because of bad polls.

Liars

Under pressure from the Democrat opposition, the White House agrees to put together an independent commission of inquiry about the CIA's successive failures regarding the weapons of mass destruction issue.

The cat among the pigeons

Former Treasury secretary Paul O'Neill publishes a book called 'The Price of Loyalty' in which he draws a vitriolic portrait of the Republican administration in place in Washington. He describes his former boss as a 'blind man surrounded by deaf people' and confirms that the Iraqi weapons of mass destruction story was a hoax made up from start to finish in order to justify the war.

PANIC AT THE WHITE HOUSE!

Spain

Al-Qaeda terrorists blow themselves up in suburban trains in and around Madrid: over 200 dead. Prime Minister José Maria Aznar is held responsible for having sent troops to Iraq and loses the Spanish legislative election that takes place just a few days afterwards.

The security fence almost finished

Vicious circle
Security fence versus terrorist attacks: Israelis and Palestinians blame each other for the failure to find a peace settlement.

Iran
The mollahs win the legislative election, having muzzled any democratic opposition prior to polling day.

MOLLAHS

OPPOSITION

A disaster waiting to happen

As foreseen by those who opposed the war in Iraq, the intervention of the American army, rather than pacifying the country, has plunged it into civil war in a state divided into Shiites, Sunnis and Kurds. They have, however, found a common enemy in the occupying American forces.

Abu Ghraib
Huge worldwide scandal after the publication of pictures taken by
American soldiers torturing Iraqis in Baghdad's infamous prison.

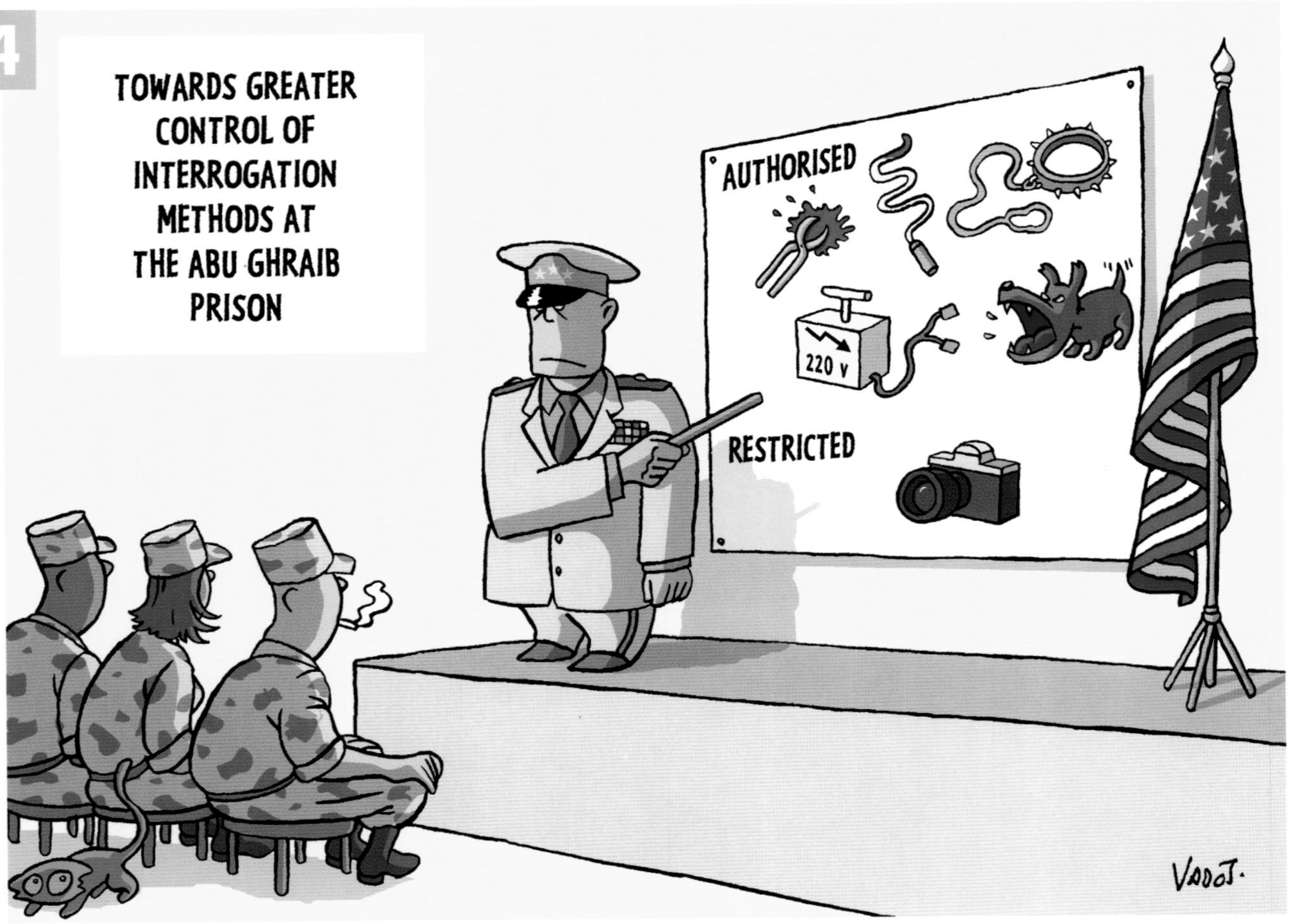
TOWARDS GREATER CONTROL OF INTERROGATION METHODS AT THE ABU GHRAIB PRISON
AUTHORISED
220 V
RESTRICTED
VADOT.

Graphic images

The publication of photos showing the tortures endured by Iraqi prisoners in the Abu Ghraib prison shock the world.

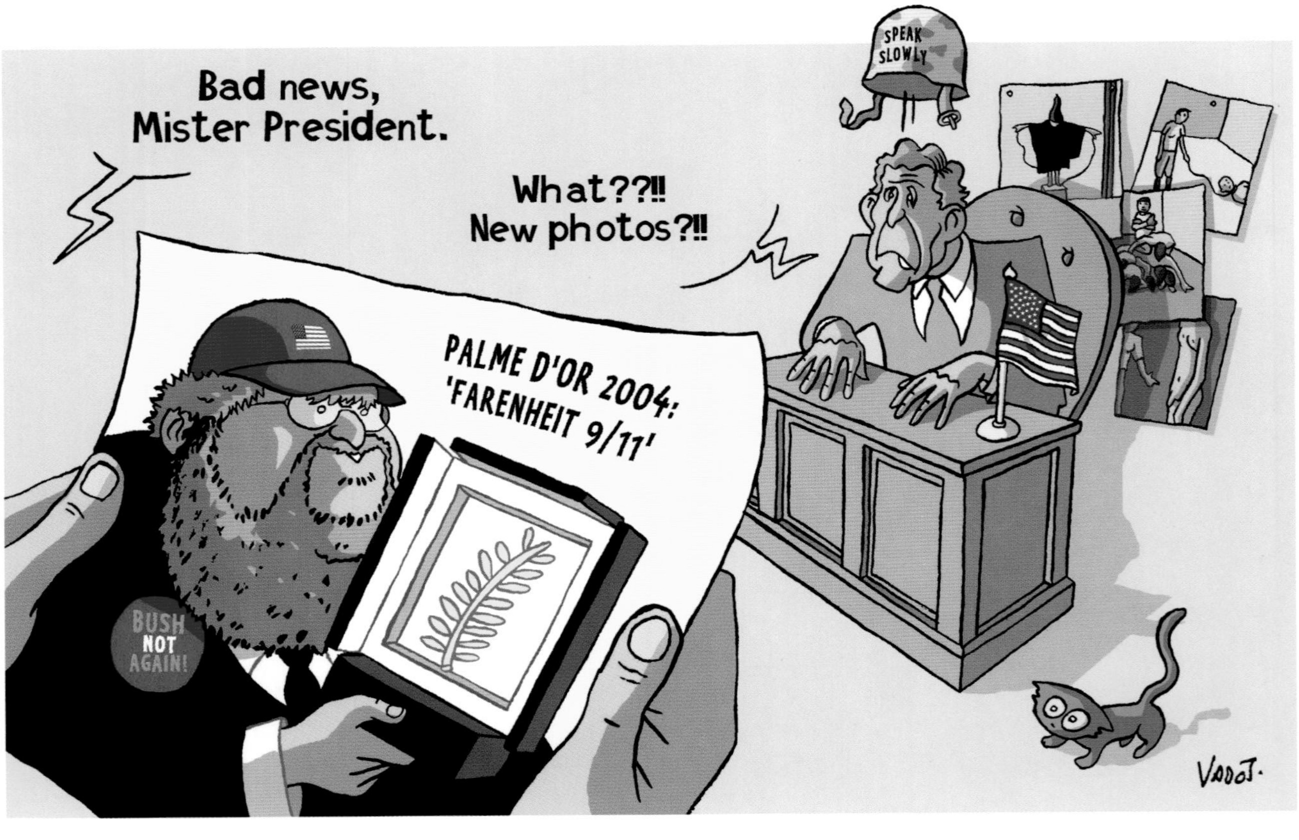
Bad news, Mister President.
What??!! New photos?!!
SPEAK SLOWLY
PALME D'OR 2004: 'FARENHEIT 9/11'
BUSH NOT AGAIN!
VADOT.

Cannes film festival

Fahrenheit 9/11, the anti-Bush lampoon produced and directed by Michael Moore, receives the Palme d'Or. The jury was presided over this year by Quentin Tarantino, director of *Reservoir Dogs.*

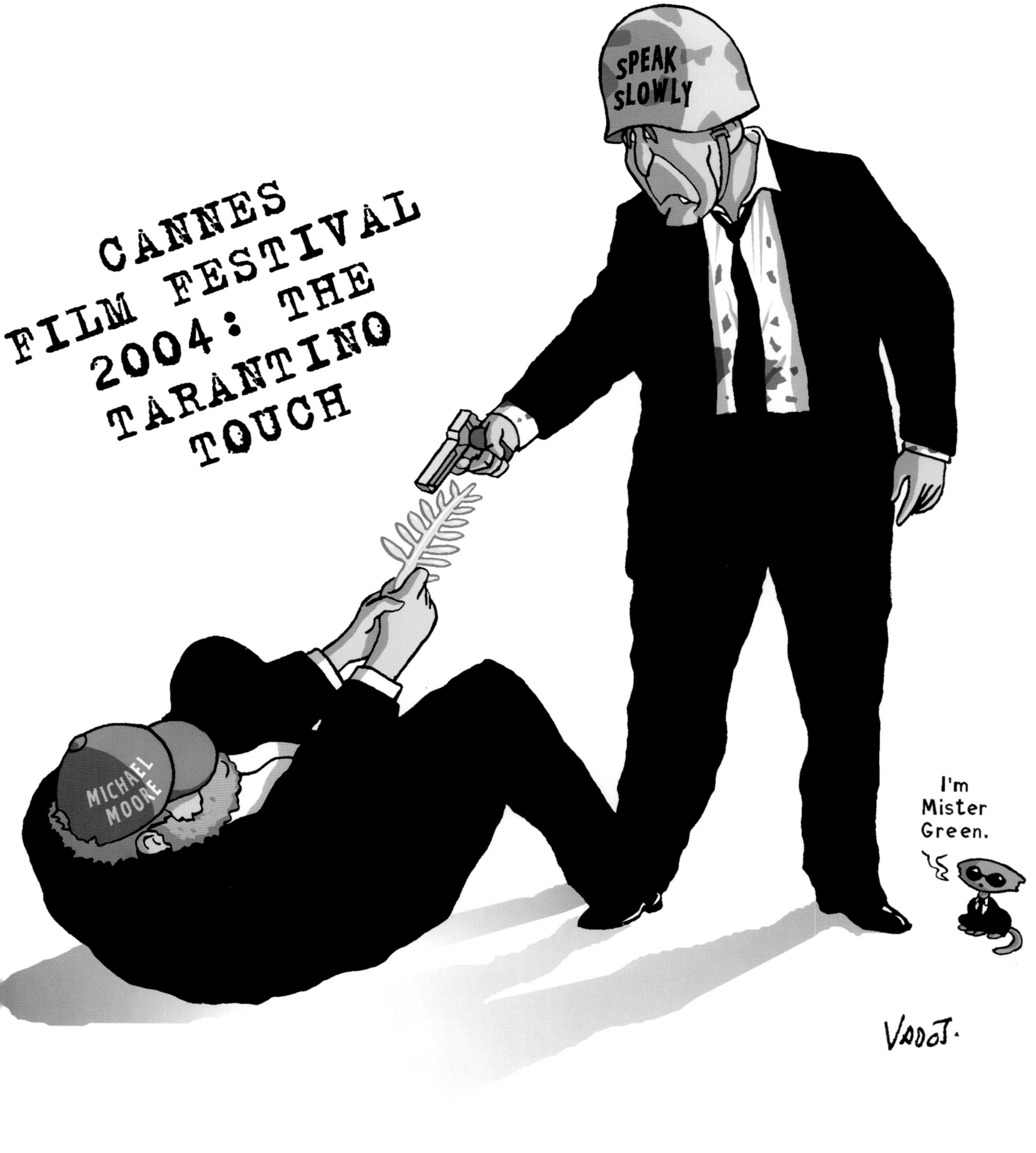
CANNES FILM FESTIVAL 2004: THE TARANTINO TOUCH
SPEAK SLOWLY
MICHAEL MOORE
I'm Mister Green.
VADOT.

Wahhabi
Al-Qaeda claims to have perpetra
a hostage taking and an attack on
sites leaving 22 dead in Saudi Arab
The Saudis are embarrassed by Islar
terrorism with which they entert
decidedly ambiguous lin

Withdrawal
Spain pulls out of the coalition in Iraq.

Globalisation
Three years after the
September 11 attacks,
Islamic terrorism has spread
all over the world.

ONE CYCLONE AFTER THE OTHER...

Catastrophes
Just over a month before the presidential election, devastating hurricanes follow one another in the Gulf of Mexico.

Ronald Reagan
Ronald Reagan, the American President who led the country at the height of the cold war and nuclear proliferation, dies at the age of 93 after a long battle with Alzheimer's disease.

Bush again

November 2004: George W. Bush beats John Kerry and is re-elected President of the United States.

Resignation

Secretary of State Colin Powell, who always embodied the moderate side of the Bush administration, steps down and is replaced by Condoleezza Rice.

Afghanistan
First democratic elections in Afghanistan since the fall of the Taliban regime.

Trial
Charles Graner, one of Abu Ghraib prison's torturers, is found
guilty by a court martial and receives a ten-year sentence.

Black list

A devastating tsunami kills 240,000 people in South East Asia, on Boxing Day 2004. A few weeks later, the United States publishes an updated list of 'Rogue States' posing a major threat to the world and supporting international terrorism. As well as the usual suspects—'Axis of Evil's' remaining two countries Iran and North Korea—the list now includes Belarus, Cuba, Burma and, more surprisingly, Zimbabwe.

To the polls

First election in Iraq since the collapse of the Saddam Hussein regime. Islamists promise voters major bloodshed, in a country under siege.

Blunder

Incredible release of Italian journalist Giuliana Sgrena, held hostage for a month in Iraq. American soldiers open fire on the car that was driving her back to the airport, shooting her in the shoulder and killing the secret agent who helped in her release. To explain their mistake, the GI's say they 'mistook the Italians for Iraqi civilians'.

Massacre

Armed with his father's gun, a teenager slaughters several classmates in a school in Minnesota. The question of the free circulation of weapons in the United States is raised yet again.

Euthanasia

George W. Bush intervenes personally to sign a law voted quickly through Congress, forbidding Terry Schiavo's husband to shut down his wife's life support system. Terry Schiavo was in an irreversible coma.

1933

'DEATH TO
JEWS!'
- Hitler -

1945

'DEATH TO
CAPITALISTS!'
- Stalin -

2001

'DEATH TO
INFIDELS!'
- Bin Laden -

2005

'DEATH TO
TERRORISTS!'
- Bush & Putin -

1945–2005
'Long Live United Europe!'
-Schröder & Chirac -

This sucks! Who do they define themselves against?

Nobody! That's their whole philosophy.

Their what?

Anniversary
May 1955–May 2005: the European Union celebrates its 50th birthday.

Terrorism
On July 7 2005, four simultaneous attacks kill 52 people on London's public transport. They were perpetrated by young British Islamists with Pakistani backgrounds, who all had spent some time in Koranic schools in Pakistan.

Just finished high school and don't know what to do with your life? Become a jihadist!

Come here young man, you whose soul is still pure. In Pakistan, our Koranic schools provide pluridisciplinary and free martyr scholarship, to make your future boom!

Huh?

Pretty straightforward, Buddy! Don't start asking questions!

First part of your training: body and soul hygiene.

Snip!

?

'Neurons reduced to a pulp, Twin Towers to dust!'

...All our brains are washed at 90° with 'Death to the West pro-active, high performance'.

Our master instructors will then teach you the basics of chemistry...

Pshiiit

The delicate art of shoe bombing...

And, of course, geography!

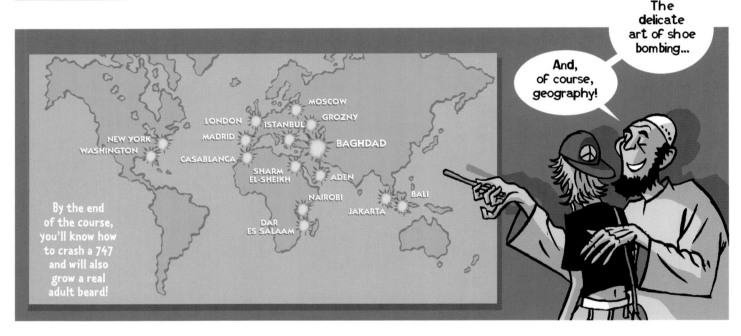

NEW YORK
WASHINGTON
LONDON
MADRID
CASABLANCA
ISTANBUL
MOSCOW
GROZNY
BAGHDAD
SHARM EL-SHEIKH
ADEN
NAIROBI
DAR ES SALAAM
JAKARTA
BALI

By the end of the course, you'll know how to crash a 747 and will also grow a real adult beard!

You'll also have a certified kamikaze degree!

SIGNED BY OSAMA BIN LADEN!

And you won't have to worry about unemployment ever again!

Cool, huh?

Yeah, well, why not...

... But what are the chicks like?

???!!

... Forget it! What's the point of going to Uni if one can't get laid!

I'll go for art instead. A lot of chicks pick art!

You bloody infidel!

Saudi Arabia
Death of King Fahd, a great friend of the Bush Family, as well as the Bin Ladens.

The hardest thing to deal with when organising a funeral is protocol.

BUSH FAMILY

BIN LADEN FAMILY

KING FAHD

CLOSE FRIENDS OF THE DECEASED

VADOT.

IRA
The Irish Republican Army lays down its weapons and renounces terrorism for good.

AL-QAEDA

Local terrorism is history...

IRA

BANKRUPT

It's become a multinationals market!

VADOT.

Iran
Ultra-conservative Mahmud Ahmadinejad is elected president. His nuclear ambitions cause huge concern within the international community.

Hiroshima

In Iraq, 40 GIs are killed in less than a week. The number of American soldiers who have died since the American invasion in March 2003 has reached 1800. Meanwhile, Washington is getting more and more bellicose towards Tehran. Iran wishes to carry on with its nuclear programme, despite warnings from the international community, especially as the world marks the 60th anniversary of Hiroshima.

Katrina
Hurricane Katrina devastates the city of New Orleans. Victims are mainly amongst the underprivileged population, mostly black. America is horrified to discover the existence of a domestic third world.

Mea Culpa
George W. Bush is accused of having underestimated the full extent of the humanitarian catastrophe caused by hurricane Katrina. He flies belatedly over the devastated areas several times.

Rita

A month after Katrina in Louisiana, a new cyclone hits Texas—George W. Bush's home state—but ends up being less destructive than expected. President Bush, criticised for not having measured the devastating impact of Katrina, flies to Texas to be present when Rita hits.

Seism

In Pakistan, Kashmir is hit by a gigantic earthquake killing at least 24,000 people in the area where Bin Laden is supposedly hiding.

Iraq

Death of the 2001st soldier in Iraq.

BUDDIES FIRST...

My dear friends...
After promoting John Bolton Ambassador to the UN, then Ben Bernanke at the FED, George W. Bush favours another one of his closest friends, appointing Harriet Miers head of the Supreme Court.

Australia
Nineteen Islamists are suspected of preparing a major chemical attack, probably targeting Sydney's nuclear reactor.

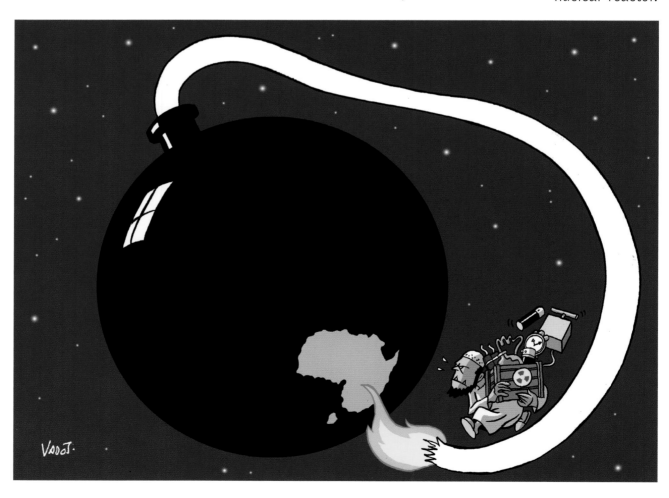

NEW CARNIVOROUS SPECIES
SPOTTED IN BORNEO

- Should we tell the WWF?
- No, the CIA.

Discovery
An unknown species of carnivorous mammal is spotted in Borneo. Meanwhile, the Qatari network al-Jazeera broadcasts a video featuring al-Qaeda's number 2, Ayman al Zawahiri, who says Osama Bin Laden is still alive and key leader of the Holy War against the West.

Optimism

George W. Bush reaffirms the war is about to be won in Iraq, even though opposition is growing within the American population. At the same time, the White House is embarrassed by revelations of phone tapping operating within the context of the 'War on Terror'.

Middle Kingdom
China becomes the fourth economic power in the world, relegating the position of France and Great Britain. However, income per inhabitant is much lower than in Western countries.

Provocation
Iranian President Mahmud Ahmadinejad says he wants to 'Wipe Israel off the map'.

Escalation
Iran again defies the international community with its programme for development of nuclear weapons. The United States considers armed intervention.

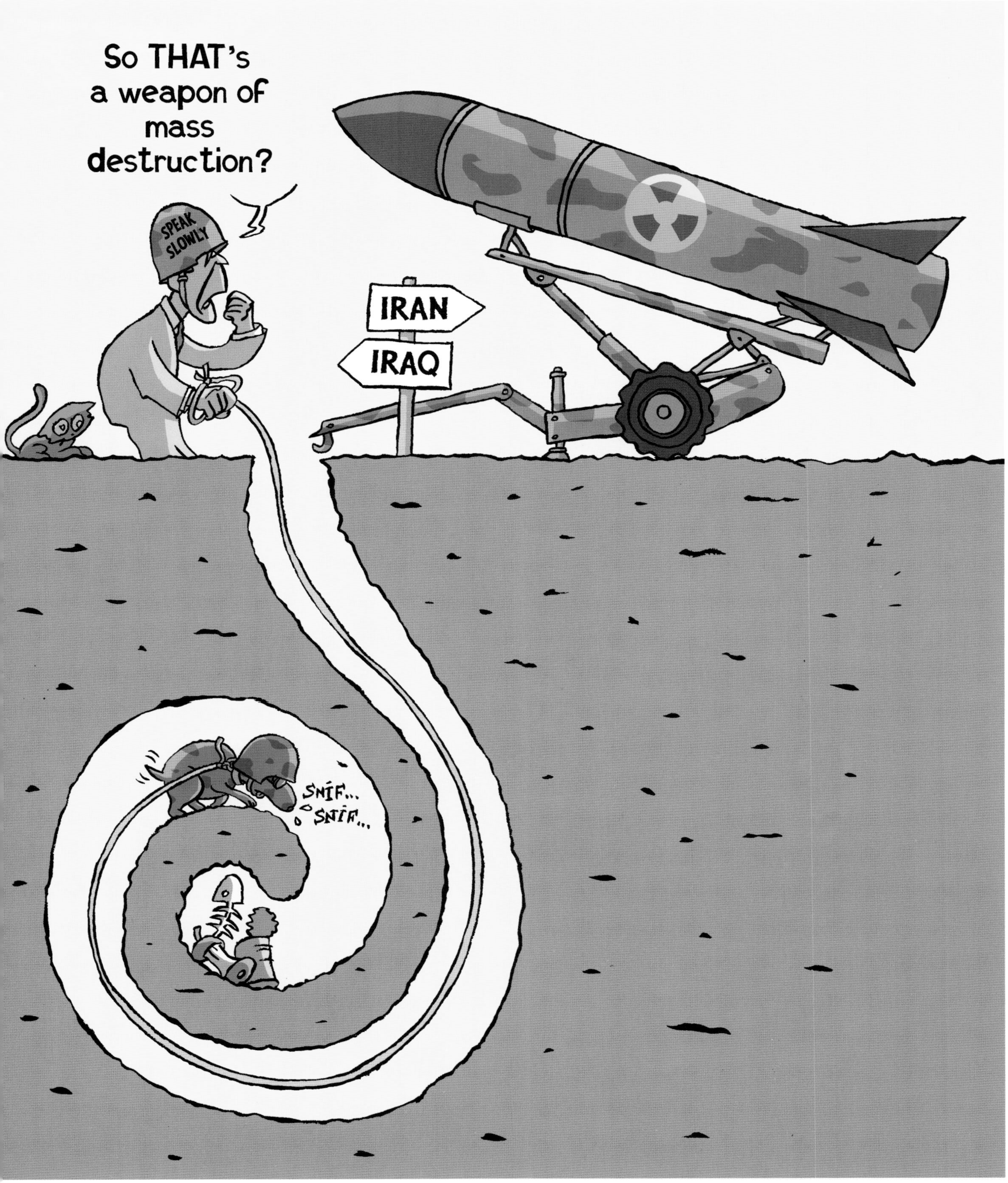
So THAT's a weapon of mass destruction?
SPEAK SLOWLY
IRAN
IRAQ
SNIF...
SNIF...

Danish cartoons crisis
Extremely violent anti-Western demonstrations take place throughout the Muslim world
following the publication in Denmark of 12 caricatures of Mohamet whose depiction
Islam forbids. Debate surrounds the role of cartoonists and freedom of speech.

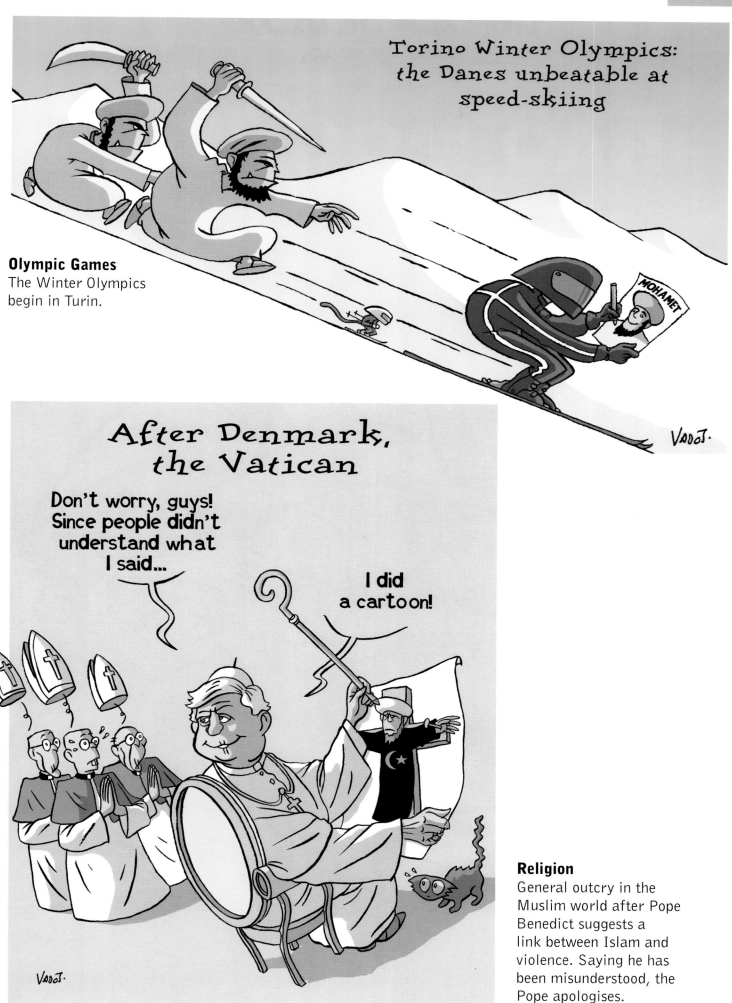

Torino Winter Olympics:
the Danes unbeatable at
speed-skiing

Olympic Games
The Winter Olympics
begin in Turin.

After Denmark,
the Vatican

Don't worry, guys!
Since people didn't
understand what
I said...

I did
a cartoon!

Religion
General outcry in the
Muslim world after Pope
Benedict suggests a
link between Islam and
violence. Saying he has
been misunderstood, the
Pope apologises.

LIVE FROM THE OSCARS

Blockbuster
Tony Blair justifies his decision to go to war against Iraq referring to his
Christian faith, as did George W. Bush. Meanwhile in Hollywood, Brokeback
Mountain, a love story between two gay cowboys, wins three Oscars.

Washington in the blizzard

One has to admit Louisiana didn't raise its hand to come and help us clear away the snow!

Bad weather
While the US East Coast is faced with a massive snowstorm, the Parliamentary commission of inquiry on Katrina is very harsh on the Bush administration, accused of not having measured the scope of the humanitarian crisis and of having waited too long to respond with adequate assistance.

NEW TORTURE METHODS REVEALED AT ABU GHRAIB PRISON IN BAGHDAD

Now you're gonna talk, or you'll be quail huntin' in Texas with Cheney!

Please no! I'll tell you everything!

Shoot me now
Further revelations leak out in the press about torture methods at the Abu Ghraib prison in 2004. Meanwhile, Vice President Dick Cheney accidentally shoots one of his friends while quail hunting in Texas, and then tries to hush up the scandal.

Suicide
Three detainees hang themselves in their cells at Guantanamo prison, where presumed
Islamist terrorists are held in custody without evidence, waiting for a trial.

Posted

Iranian President Mahmud Ahmadinejad writes to George W. Bush in an attempt to reduce the tension concerning Tehran's nuclear programme. In his letter he repeats his belief in religious values.

Zacharias Mussawi

The Frenchman, condemned to a life sentence for his alleged role in the September 11 attacks, retracts his guilty plea and protests his innocence.

Doping

The key favourites in the Tour de France are excluded from the competition the day before the start, having been compromised in another drugs scandal. In Lebanon, as the war intensifies between Israel and Hezbollah, the time has come to question which countries are responsible for financing and arming the belligerents.

CRAZY HOW ONE CAN MANIPULATE IMAGES THANKS TO MODERN COMPUTER TECHNOLOGY

Retouching
A Reuters photographer is sacked for having digitally retouched pictures he took
during bombings in Beirut, adding smoke to make things look more dramatic.
The propaganda war is intense on both the Israeli and the Hezbollah side.

Stem cells

Israel continues to bomb Lebanon, implicitly supported by Washington. Meanwhile in the United States, President Bush vetoes an attempt to pass a law authorising embryonic research on stem cells, on the pretext of ethical reasons.

Nuclear crisis
Renewed concern on behalf of the international community in connection with North Korea's military nuclear programme, North Korea being one of the poorest countries in the world and one of the last remaining Stalinist regimes.

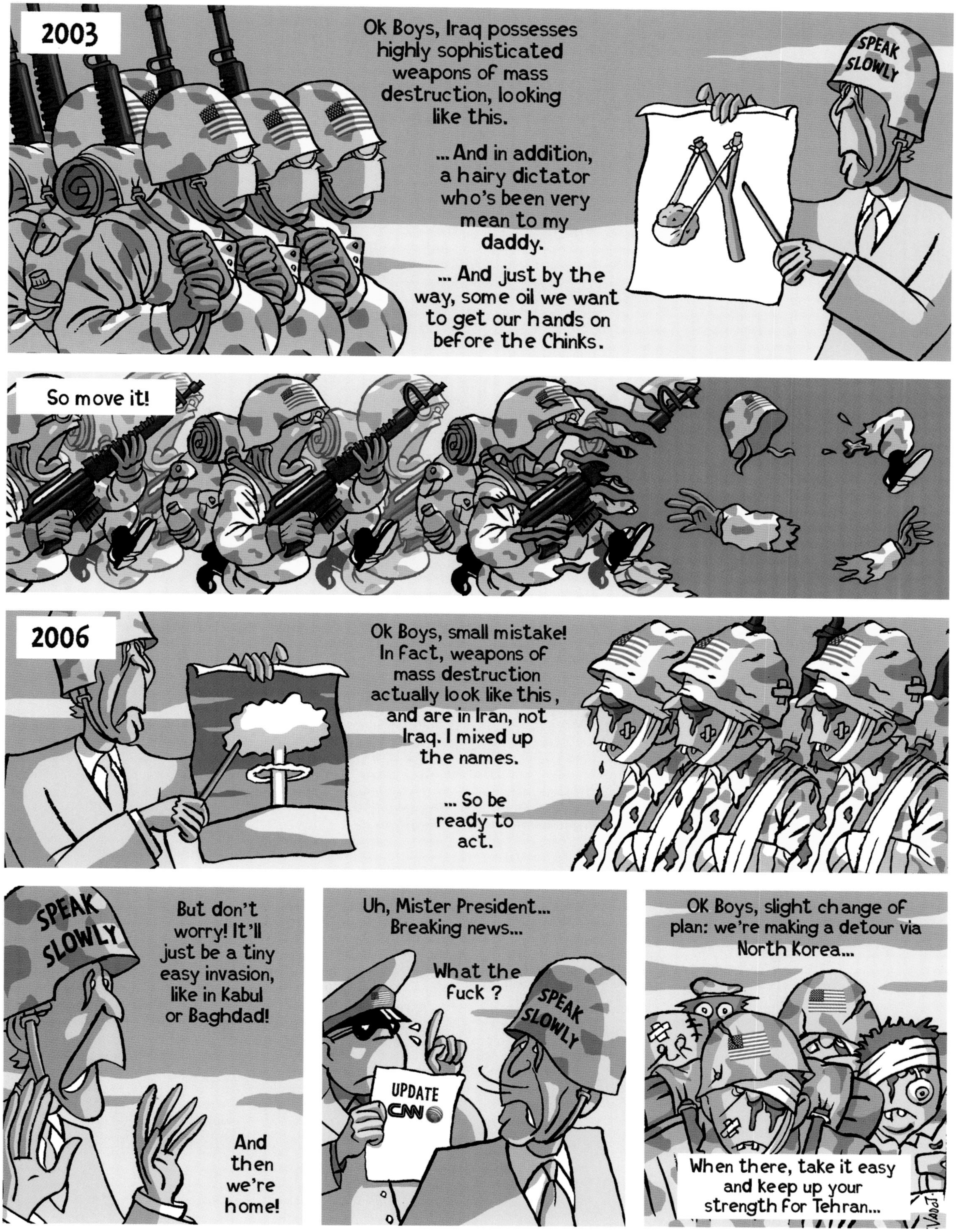
2003
Ok Boys, Iraq possesses highly sophisticated weapons of mass destruction, looking like this.
... And in addition, a hairy dictator who's been very mean to my daddy.
... And just by the way, some oil we want to get our hands on before the Chinks.
SPEAK SLOWLY
So move it!
2006
Ok Boys, small mistake! In fact, weapons of mass destruction actually look like this, and are in Iran, not Iraq. I mixed up the names.
... So be ready to act.
SPEAK SLOWLY
But don't worry! It'll just be a tiny easy invasion, like in Kabul or Baghdad!
And then we're home!
Uh, Mister President... Breaking news...
What the fuck ?
SPEAK SLOWLY
UPDATE
CNN
OK Boys, slight change of plan: we're making a detour via North Korea...
When there, take it easy and keep up your strength for Tehran...
VADOT

Remembrance
September 11's fifth anniversary.

Bin Laden
New claim that al-Qaeda's leader is thought to have died from typhoid fever.

Intimidations
The American administration sets up a software programme that can analyse the content of journalists' articles in order to spot those who criticise Bush's policies.

Immigration
The Chicanos—the Spanish-speaking minority representing 10% of the entire American population—demonstrate in order to obtain more recognition and legal rights.

Population growth
The American population reaches 300 million inhabitants, thanks to the increase in the Hispanic minority that is likely to become the majority in about a hundred years.

generation

r Chavez in Venezuela, Morales in Bolivia and Lula in
zil, Ecuador elects a left-wing president, Raphael Correa.

THE UNITED STATES OF SOUTH AMERICA

Venezuela

Anti-Bush president Hugo Chavez revokes the concession of opposition private network RCTV. The poor people living in the 'barrios' who were very keen on the soppy soaps provided by RCTV are in disbelief.

Islam

In England, Islamic women living in Lancashire will now have the right to wear a burqa during their stay in hospital.

Anti-Semitism

Iranian president Mahmud Ahmadinejad organises a conference in Tehran questioning the real existence of the holocaust and invites French revisionist Robert Faurisson, as well as ultra-orthodox anti-Zionist Jews and Klu Klux Klan leaders. Ahmadinejad predicts the collapse of Israel, 'Like it happened to the Soviet Union'.

2006

Washington
The Democrats win the US mid-term elections. George W. Bush and the Republicans are paying the price of the unpopular war in Iraq.

Action painting

140 Million $ 2000 Billion $

'N°5' JACKSON POLLOCK USA -1948	'N°3000-GIS KILLED SO FAR' GEORGE W. BUSH - IRAQ 2003 - 20??

Contemporary art
'N°5', from abstract painter Jackson Pollock sells at auction for 140
million dollars, becoming the most expensive painting ever. At the same
time, the death toll of US soldiers killed in Iraq reaches 3000.

Recommendations

Conclusions of an Iraq Study Group co-chaired by James Baker, Bush Senior's former Chief of Staff, completely disavow George W. Bush's policy. The report also suggests the inclusion of Syria and Iran in peace talks to try to pacify the region.

Execution

Saddam Hussein is sentenced to death for the massacre of the population of the Kurdish village of Hallabjah, and hanged in Baghdad on Eid celebration day.

Good manners
After Saddam Hussein, two of his fellow-accused are executed by hanging, one of them being beheaded in the process. Condoleezza Rice asks for future executions to be 'more humane'.

Since we've been asked to help out Americans in Iraq, we're practising sovereign country occupation!

Lebanon

Hezbollah, financed by Iran and Syria, demonstrates in Beirut against the pro-US government.

Ok boys, I have a new killer plan!

Heads, I win, tails, you lose!

Stubbornness

Going against recommendations drawn by Congress's report on the war in Iraq, President Bush sends in 21,500 more GIs and bans Syria and Iran from negotiations.

CONDI IN JERUSALEM

Peace talks

Condoleezza Rice goes to Jerusalem to work out a lasting resolution that could help the peace process between Israel and the Palestinians. The Bush Administration has ignored the Middle East conflict for a long time, focusing on Iraq instead.

New face

Barack Obama, born to an American mother and a Kenyan father, formally announces his candidacy for the 2008 presidential election.

Climate change

International conferences on global warming, first in Paris then in Brussels and finally in Bangkok.

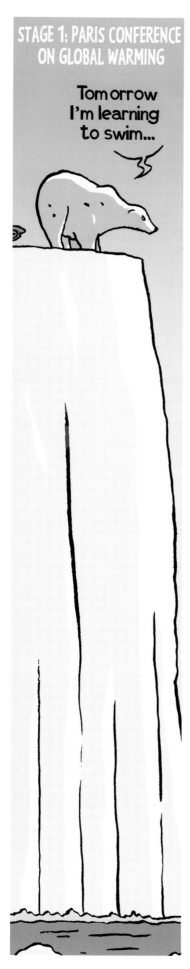

STAGE 1: PARIS CONFERENCE ON GLOBAL WARMING

STAGE 2: BRUSSELS CONFERENCE ON GLOBAL WARMING

STAGE 3: BANGKOK CONFERENCE ON GLOBAL WARMING

STAGE 4...

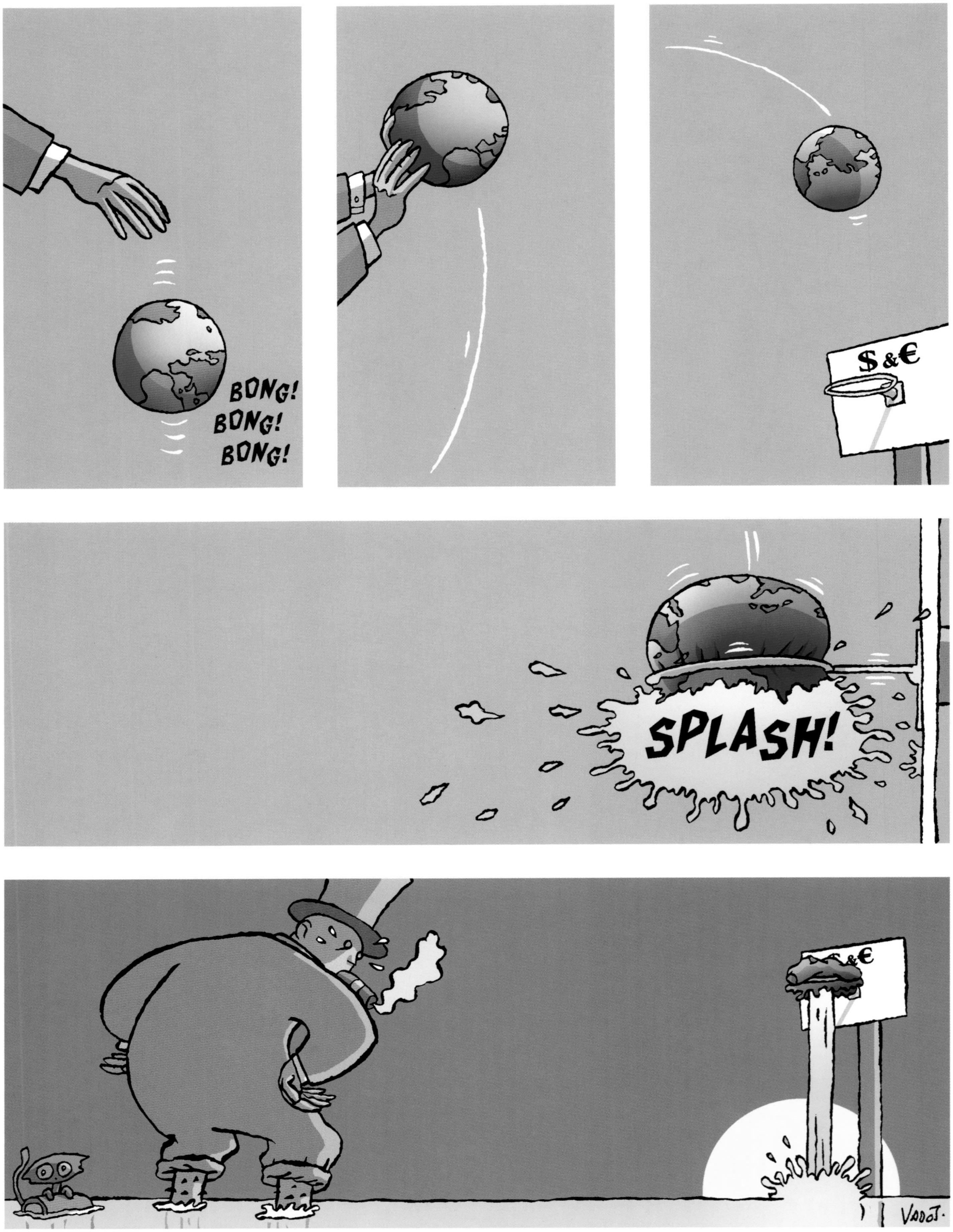
BONG!
BONG!
BONG!
$&€
SPLASH!
$&€
VADOT.

Such An Inconvenient Truth

'An Inconvenient Truth'
Al Gore's movie is
released worldwide.

Leonardo Di Caprio
The star of 'Titanic' and long-
time environmental activist,
presents 'The 11th Hour', his
documentary on global warming,
at the Cannes Film Festival.

ENVIRONMENTAL DAMAGE UNDER GEORGE W. BUSH'S PRESIDENCY.
EXAMPLE: DEFORESTATION

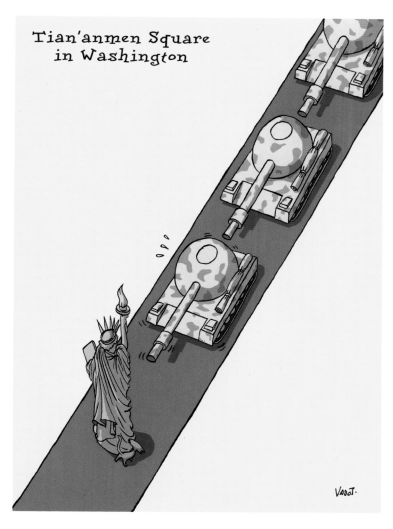

Disowning

American Congress votes against President Bush's plan to send more troops to Iraq, a nonbinding but symbolic action taken by Democrats, who have the majority.

U-turn

Britain is about to withdraw its troops from Iraq.

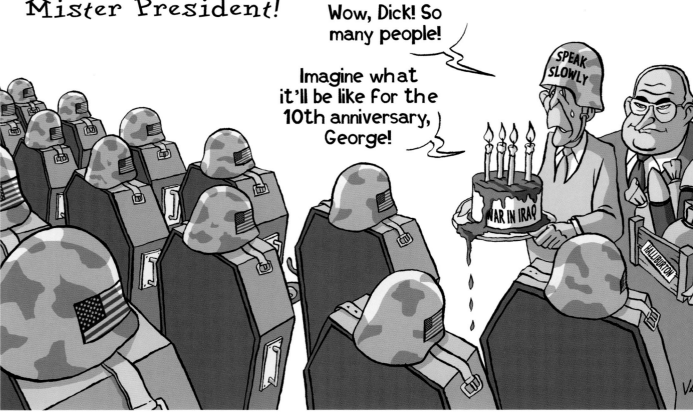

Iraq
Commemorating the fourth anniversary of the war.

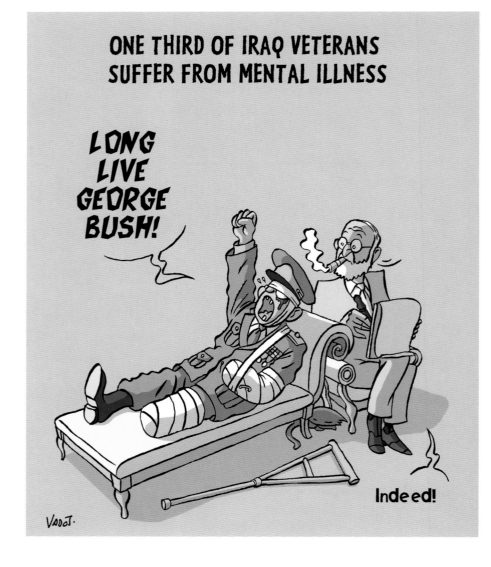

Ingratitude
An American study reveals that many Iraq veterans do not receive proper treatment upon their return, many of them suffering from mental illness.

Big rock
American scientists are concerned about a large asteroid that could hit the Earth in less than 30 years. In the Middle East, Washington is now seriously thinking of bombing Iranian military sites in order to destroy Tehran's nuclear capabilities.

Iraq
American and Iranian diplomats meet in Baghdad to try to improve the situation.

Ahmadinejad
Iran wants its nuclear programme to reach an 'industrial level'.

Maghreb
Terrorist attacks in Algeria and Morocco. In Algiers, suicide bombers blow themselves up on the street, claiming the lives of more than 30 people. Algerians fear Islamic terrorist reprisals.

Wolfowitz
Paul Wolfowitz, Pentagon former number two and instigator of the war in Iraq, resigns after facing a scandal within the World Bank which he has headed since January 2005. Despite his so-called priority to fight corruption, he awarded a $US60,000 salary increase to his partner Shaha Riza, the World Bank communications advisor. Meanwhile, George Bush asks Congress for further funding for the wars in Iraq and Afghanistan.

Plame-gate

Lewis 'Scooter' Libby, Vice President Dick Cheney's ex-chief of staff, is found guilty of obstruction of justice and perjury in the 'Plame-gate'. CIA undercover agent Valerie Plame's identity was revealed thanks to a leak from the White House in 2003, after her husband, ex-ambassador Joseph Wilson, publicly accused the Bush Administration of twisting CIA intelligence in order to exaggerate Saddam Hussein's regime's military capabilities.

THIS CARTOON IS PROUDLY BROUGHT TO YOU BY CHARLTON HESTON AND THE NATIONAL RIFLE ASSOCIATION

Carnage

A mad gunman kills more than 30 people at Virginia Tech University. The question of the free circulation of guns in America is raised again. But the National Rifle Association—one of the Republican Party's major sponsors—still firmly blocks any attempt to change the law.

HOW TO SPOT FUTURE MAD GUNMEN?

Cho Seung-Hui
The 23-year-old Virginia Tech murderer was known for previous psychiatric incidents. Some of his teachers had pointed out his 'unstable' mind. In a pre-recorded statement the killer referred to Jesus' sacrifice.

Great Britain
Tony Blair officially announces he will step down as Prime Minister at the end of June 2007.

Gordon Brown
Tony Blair makes his last trip to Baghdad as Prime Minister. His successor at Downing Street is
likely to inflect his country's policy in Iraq and withdraw British troops.

New balance of world power...

Darfur

George W. Bush puts pressure on the Sudanese regime in order to stop the genocide in Darfur. China, well established in the area searching for oil, disapproves. Later on, a conference is held in Paris, including the United States, Europe, Russia, the UN and China, who all agree to say that the situation is intolerable. But the use of force against the Sudani regime isn't agreed upon yet.

The Paris conference on Darfur was a great success.

The international community managed to reach an historical consensus.

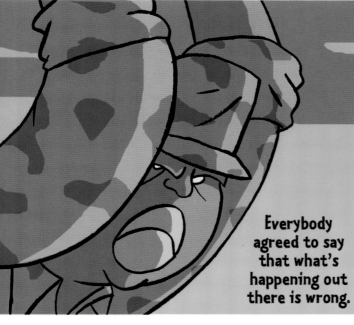

Everybody agreed to say that what's happening out there is wrong.

Well, that's all.

The G8 summit behind the scenes

Ok boys,
Once you've finished being childish, could you join us for discussions on climate change?

Cold War

Fierce tensions between Russians and Americans regarding their anti-missile shields, prior to the G8 summit organised in Germany, where world leaders will discuss climate change issues. Vladimir Putin threatens to point his missiles towards Europe if America carries out its project to establish theirs in Eastern Europe.

A Pole wakes up after spending 19 years in a coma...

What a shame! After all this time, nothing has changed!

Back to the future

A Polish worker wakes up after spending almost two decades in a coma. Back then, in 1988, the Cold War still prevailed.

A CIA AIRCRAFT USED FOR TRANSFERRING ALLEGED TERRORISTS TO OVERSEAS SECRET INTERROGATION CENTRES IS HIDDEN IN THIS CARTOON. CAN YOU FIND IT?

'Ghost flights'

New evidence on 'torture flights': The CIA is accused of having set up secret prisons outside America so it could use interrogation techniques amounting to torture which are illegal in the United States. Prisoners were flown to those secret prisons throughout the world, including European countries such as Romania and Poland.

Patriot Act

In a major setback for Bush's policies in the war on terrorism adopted after the September 11 attacks, Ali Saleh Kahlah al-Marri, a Qatari national suspected of being an al-Qaeda operative, is set free. He was the only person being held in the United States under the Patriot Act legislation as an 'enemy combatant', with no evidence of guilt.

'The government cannot subject al-Marri to indefinite military detention. For in the United States, the military cannot seize and imprison civilians—let alone imprison them indefinitely,' says the court before ordering his release from military custody.

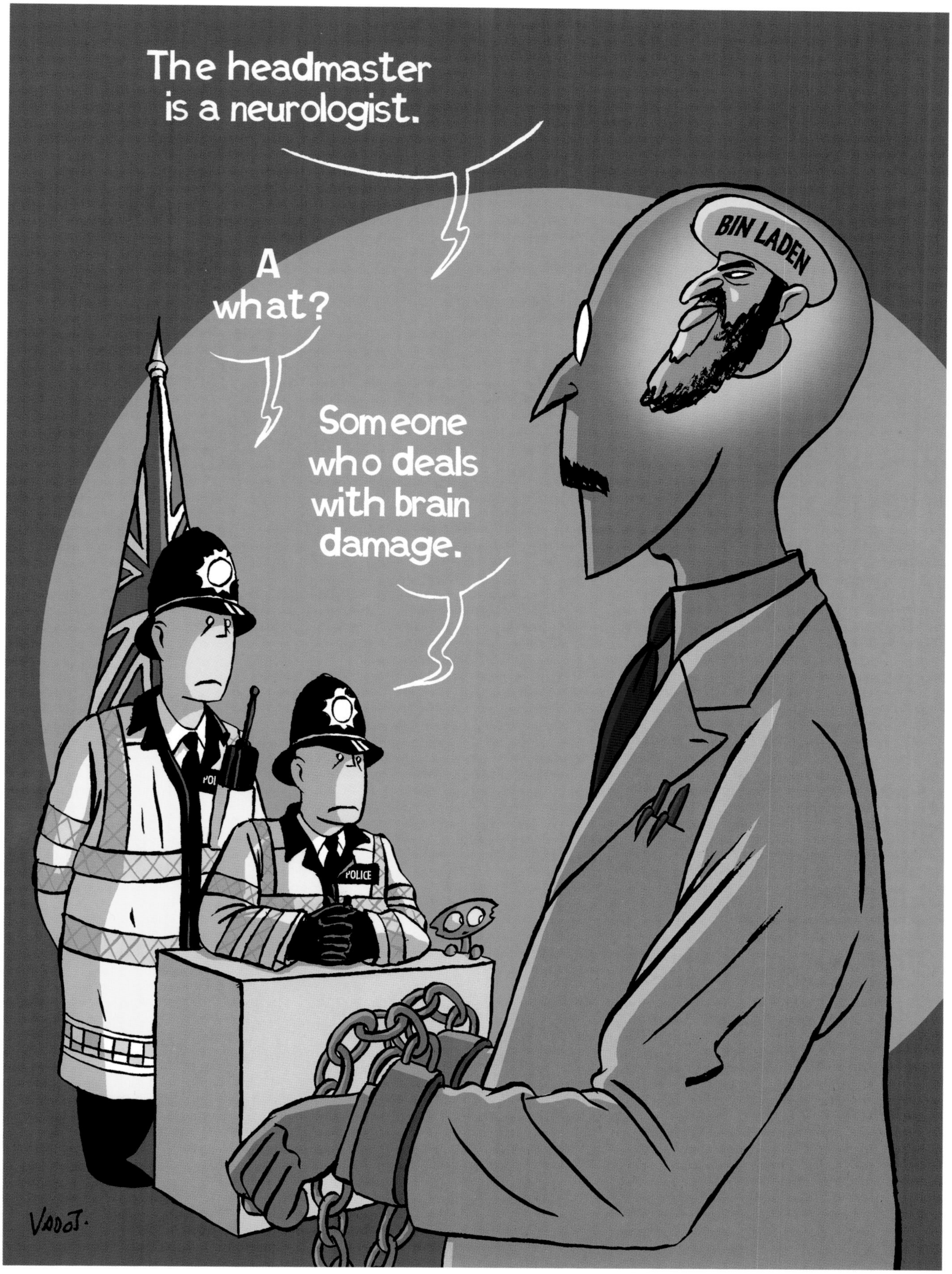
The headmaster is a neurologist.
A what?
Someone who deals with brain damage.
BIN LADEN
POLICE
VADOT.

Neurologist

Foiled terrorist attacks in London, just two years after the bombings that killed 52 people. The operation headmaster is a 27-year-old Jordan neurologist.

Acknowledgements

Nicolas Vadot would like to thank...

My translation team: Jean Willoughby, Catherine and Susan Vadot; Fiona Schultz and everyone at New Holland as well as my agents in Australia, Clare Calvet and Xavier Waterkeyn, for trusting me; Serge Wittock, the ultimate go-between; Bob Stebbings for his New York City perspectives; www.nicolasvadot.com webmaster Fabrice Grenson for his hard work; former *Le Vif/L'Express* editor-in-chief Jacques Gevers, who taught me everything; Vincent Baudoux, for helping me make the right choices a very long time ago; and, last but not least, George W. Bush himself for being such an inexhaustable source of inspiration.

To Ella Vadot...

Nicolas Vadot website: www.nicolasvadot.com
First published in Australia in 2007 by
New Holland Publishers (Australia) Pty Ltd
Sydney • Auckland • London • Cape Town

1/66 Gibbes Street Chatswood NSW 2067 Australia
218 Lake Road Northcote Auckland New Zealand
86 Edgware Road London W2 2EA United Kingdom
80 McKenzie Street Cape Town 8001 South Africa

A record of this book is held at the National Library of Australia.

ISBN 9781741106213

Publisher: Fiona Schultz
Designer: Natasha Hayles
Production Manager: Linda Bottari
Printer: Power Printing Products Ltd.

10 9 8 7 6 5 4 3 2 1